Emotions

for kids age 1-3

By Dayna Martin

e ENGAGE BOOKS

Mailing address
PO BOX 4608
Main Station Terminal
349 West Georgia Street
Vancouver, BC
Canada, V6B 4A1

www.engagebooks.ca

Written & compiled by: Dayna Martin
Edited & designed by: A.R. Roumanis
Photos supplied by: Shutterstock

FIRST EDITION / FIRST PRINTING

LIBRARY AND ARCHIVES CANADA CATALOGUING IN PUBLICATION

Martin, Dayna, 1983–, author
    Emotions for kids age 1-3 / written by Dayna Martin ; edited by A.R. Roumanis.

(Engage early readers : children's learning books)
Issued in print and electronic formats.
ISBN 978-1-77226-065-6 (paperback). –
ISBN 978-1-77226-066-3 (bound). –
ISBN 978-1-77226-067-0 (pdf). –
ISBN 978-1-77226-068-7 (epub). –
ISBN 978-1-77226-069-4 (kindle)

1. Emotions – Juvenile literature.
I. Roumanis, A. R., editor
II. Title.

BF561.M38 2015   J152.4   C2015-903406-X
                                                          C2015-903407-8

Emotions

for kids age 1-3

Engage Early Readers

Children's Learning Books

by Dayna Martin

ENGAGE BOOKS / VANCOUVER

3

Anger

4

Brave

Love

6

Jealous

7

Scared

8

Pride

Frustration

10

Shock

11

Grumpy

12

Shy

13

Annoyed

14

Hope

15

Sad

16

Sleepy

17

Silly

Guilt

Judgement

19

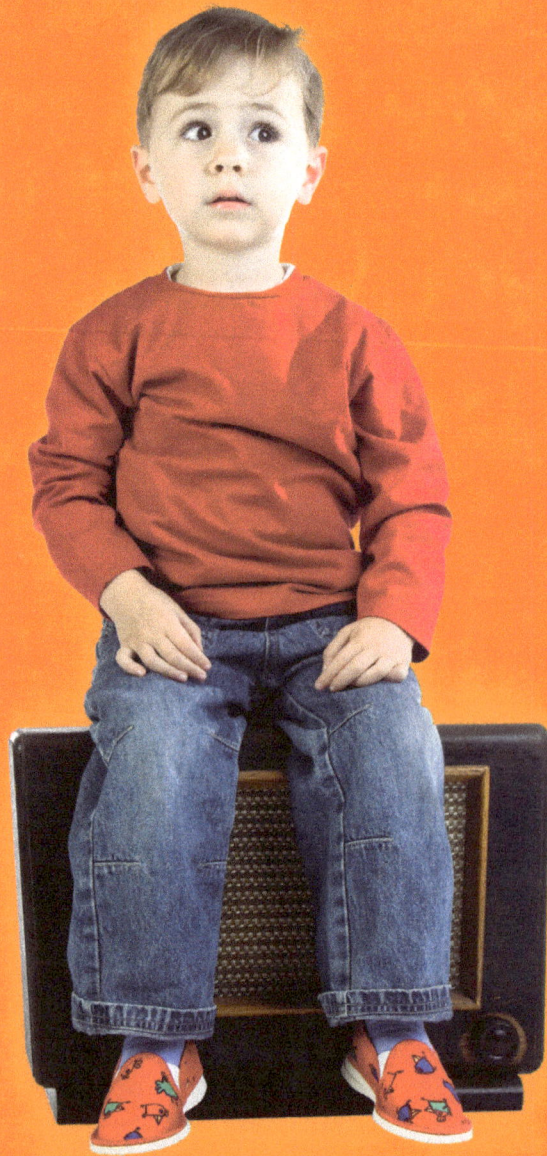

Nervous

20

Pouty

21

Wonder

Surprise

Depressed

24

Disgust

25

Hurt

Happy

Bored

Sorry

Emotions activity

Do you know what these emotions and expressions are called? Can you find **happy, love, surprise, sleepy, scared, anger, brave, sad,** and **shock**? Match the names to the pictures below.

Answer: shock

Answer: scared

Answer: sleepy

Answer: surprise

Answer: brave

Answer: happy

Answer: anger

Answer: sad

Answer: love

30

Colors for Kids
age 1-3

Yellow Fish
Orange Flower
Purple Eggplant
White Bear
Red Fire Hydrant
Blue Hat
Pink Pig
Green Lego

Opposites for Kids
age 1-3

Out
In
Long
Short
On
Off
Up
Down
Big
Small
Slow
Fast
Old
New
Front
Back

Actions for Kids
age 1-3

Eat
Jump
Crawl
Brush
Wave
Kick
Swim
Ride

Sizes for Kids
age 1-3

Small
Medium
Large
Small
Large
Medium
Small
Medium
Large
Medium
Small
Large
Small
Medium
Medium
Large
Small
Large
Medium
Small

Numbers for Kids
age 1-3

4 Raspberries
7 Rubber Ducks
2 Cars
8 Presents
5 Cups
1 Bowl
6 Balloons
3 Pickles

ABCs for Kids
age 1-3

Fox
Lion
Vulture
Tiger
Bear
Rabbit
Dog
Cat

Shapes for Kids
age 1-3

Starfish
Clock
Leaf
Chalkboard
ABC
Door
Rings
Cracker
Pizza

Sounds for Kids
age 1-3

Ribbit
Moo
Vroom
Flush
Clap
Ring
Roar
Cock-a-doodle-doo

Sports for Kids
age 1-3

Badminton
Basketball
Baseball
Volleyball
Soccer
Golf
Tennis

www.ingramcontent.com/pod-product-compliance
Lightning Source LLC
Chambersburg PA
CBHW060800150426

42813CB00058B/2781